Nelson Comprehension

Pupil Book

Red

Sarah Lindsay
Series Editor: John Jackman

OXFORD
UNIVERSITY PRESS

Great Clarendon Street, Oxford, OX2 6DP, United Kingdom

Oxford University Press is a department of the University of Oxford. It furthers the University's objective of excellence in research, scholarship, and education by publishing worldwide. Oxford is a registered trade mark of Oxford University Press in the UK and in certain other countries

Text © Sarah Lindsay 2014
Illustrations © Oxford University Press 2014

The moral rights of the authors have been asserted

First published by Nelson Thornes Ltd in 2009

British Library Cataloguing in Publication Data
Data available

978-1-4085-0545-8

10 9 8 7 6 5

Printed in Spain

Acknowledgements

Cover: Iole Rosa (c/o Beehive Illustration)
Illustrations: Neil Chapman, Russ Daff, Pascale Lafond, Gustavo Mazali, Brenda McKetty, Pedro Penizzotto, Mike Phillips, Iole Rosa, Simon Rumble, Elena Selivanova, Pete Smith, Matt Ward (all c/o Beehive Illustration) and Chris Masters
Photography: Heather Gunn (www.heathergunnphotography.co.uk) © Oxford University Press
Page make-up: Topics the Creative Partnership, Exeter

The author and publisher are grateful to the following for permission to reproduce copyright material:

[Unit 1 Teach] extract from D. King-Smith, *Sophie's Adventures*, reproduced with kind permission of A P Watt Ltd on behalf of Fox Busters Ltd; [Unit 3 Talk] extract from Mary and Rich Chamberlin, *Mama Panya's Pancakes*, Barefoot Books (www.barefootbooks.com); [Unit 5 Teach] extract 'Cookie Sensations' from T. Mitton, Senses Poems, 1996, OUP granted by David Higham Associates; [Unit 5 Write] *I Like* © Moira Andrew, reproduced with author's permission; [Unit 6 Teach] Extract from *Prince Cinders* by Babette Cole, HamishHamilton,1987, Reproduced by permissions of Penguin Books Ltd; [Unit 8 Teach] Extract from *The Sandcastle* by M.P. Robertson, published by Frances Lincoln Ltd, © 2001 reproduced by kind permission of Frances Lincoln Ltd.; [Unit 8 Write] Extract and illustrations from J. Kerr, *The Tiger Who Came To Tea*, reprinted by permission of HarperCollins Publishers Ltd. © Judith Kerr 1968; [Unit 10 Teach] Cows, © James Reeves from *Complete Poems for Children* (Faber Finds) reprinted by permission of the James Reeves Estate; [Unit 10 Write] *The Cow in the Storm* © Richard Edwards, reproduced with author's permission.

Although we have made every effort to trace and contact all copyright holders before publication this has not been possible in all cases. If notified, the publisher will rectify any errors or omissions at the earliest opportunity.

Links to third party websites are provided by Oxford in good faith and for information only. Oxford disclaims any responsibility for the materials contained in any third party website referenced in this work.

Contents

Scope and sequence

Unit	Unit name	Unit focus	Text type / genre
1	Familiar settings	Exploring events and characters in a setting	Stories with familiar settin
2	Labels and captions	Looking at labels and captions	Labels, lists and captions
3	Stories from home and far away	Recognising predictable, patterned language	Stories from a range of cultures; texts using patterned and predictable language
4	Instructions	Understanding instructions	Instructions
5	Using the senses	Exploring senses through poetry	Poetry
6	Traditional and fairy tales	Exploring characters and events in traditional stories	Traditional stories
7	Recounts	Understanding recounts and ordering events	Recounts
8	Fantasy worlds	Exploring characters and events in fantasy stories	Fantasy stories
9	Information texts	Understanding information texts	Information texts
10	Pattern and rhyme	Exploring pattern and rhyme in poetry	Poetry

Teach/Talk extract	Write extract	Comprehension skills
Sophie's Snail, Dick King-Smith	Tim's Bedtime	Literal Evaluation – empathy / prior knowledge Visualisation
Farm fun map	Adam's visit	Literal Inference Evaluation – opinion
Mama Panya's Pancakes, Mary and Rich Chamberlin	It Sounds Like An Owl, John Jackman	Literal Inference Analysis – text structure
Banana split	Time for a Drink	Literal Inference Summarising Analysis – text structure
Cookie Sensations, Tony Mitton	I Like, Moira Andrew	Literal Visualisation Evaluation – personal experience
Prince Cinders, Babette Cole	Cinderella	Literal Inference Evaluation – opinion
Our visit to the dinosaurs	My naughty dog!	Literal Visualisation
The Sandcastle, M.P. Robertson	The Tiger Who Came to Tea, Judith Kerr	Literal Visualisation
Being a friend	Sorting out an argument	Analysis – text structure Literal Inference Evaluation – previous experience
Cows, James Reeves	The Cow in the Storm, Richard Edwards	Literal Inference Analysis – language use Evaluation – opinion experience

Familiar settings

▶ **Explaining events and characters in a story**

Sophie's Snail

- Who is the main character in the story?

- When does the story happen?

- Where does the story happen?

- What happens to the snail?

Sophie's snail is sucked down the plug hole.

- How do you think Sophie feels?
- Why does Sophie feel like this?

What do you think happens next?

7

Tim's Bedtime

This is what I do when I go to bed.

I fill the sink with water.

I wash my face.

I brush my teeth.

I pull out the plug and then go to bed.

Copy the right answers.

1 What does Tim do first?
He washes his face.   He fills the sink.

2 Does Tim wash his face before he brushes his teeth?
Yes   No

3 What does Tim do after he brushes his teeth?
He pulls out the plug.   He washes his face.

What do you do when you get ready for bed?

4 Write three things you do before you get into bed.

9

Farm Fun

CAFÉ

The café sells sandwiches, drinks and sweets

Ice cream Cold drinks Tea

PETS CORNER

Playground

A chance to feed and pet some rabbits, goats and sheep

Cows

Ponies

Goats

Sheep

Hens

Start

shop open

WELCOME

You can buy toys and small gifts from the shop

Farm Walk
The walk will take one hour

Car park

- What can you buy from the shop?

- Where can you buy sweets?

- What animals can you feed at Pets Corner?

- How many animals do you see on the Farm Walk?

Look at the Farm Walk on the map.

You would like your mum to take you on the Farm Walk. Tell her about it.

- How long does it take?

- Where does the path lead?

- What animals will you see?

11

Adam's visit

Adam eats his lunch.

Adam looks at the cows.

1 Where does Adam sit to eat his sandwiches?

Adam sits outside the café.
Adam sits inside the café.

2 Which animals does Adam feed?

Adam feeds the sheep.
Adam feeds the goats.

3 What does Adam do at the playground?

Adam plays on the slide.
Adam plays on the swings.

4 Two pictures need a sentence.

Write a sentence for each picture.

Write what Adam is doing.

Don't forget to use a capital letter and a full stop in your sentences!

5 Do you think Adam enjoyed his day out?

Write a sentence saying why.

13

Mama Panya's Pancakes
A village tale from Kenya

Adika, we have to go to market.

I'm two steps ahead of you!

Are you making pancakes Mama?

Yes.

Pancakes tonight?

I'll be there.

I'm two steps ahead.

Will you come?

- Where are Mama and Adika going?

- Is Adika ready when Mama wants to go?

- What is Mama cooking for tea?

- How many friends do Adika and Mama meet?

Adika keeps saying
'I'm two steps ahead'.

- What is Adika like?

- Why do you think the author keeps using this phrase?

I'm two steps ahead.

Mama is looking worried in the last picture.

Why do you think she looks worried?

15

It Sounds Like An Owl

Howl ... Howl ...
"What's that sound? What's that loud sound?" said Ben.
"It sounds like an owl. It must be an owl," said Pen. "Go to sleep, Ben!"
"It's not an owl. Owls don't howl!" said Ben.

Howl ... Howl ...
"What's that sound? What's that loud sound?" said Ben.
"It sounds like a cow. It must be a cow," said Sue. "Go to sleep, Ben!"
"It's not a cow. Cows don't howl!" said Ben.

Howl ... Howl ...
"It's Spot! It's Spot! Shut up Spot and go back to the house!"

Howl! Howl!

Copy and finish the sentences.

1 Ben is worried by the _____.

owl   howl

howl

2 Pen thinks the howl is an _____.

cow   owl

3 Sue tells Ben to go to _____.

lie down   sleep

4 It is _____ howling.

Spot   Ben

5 This story has a pattern.

- Copy a line that is repeated in the story.
- How many lines are repeated?

Banana split

You will need:

1 banana

2 scoops of ice cream

 chocolate sauce

a few strawberries

some chocolate chips

What to do:

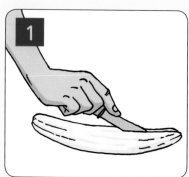

Your banana split is now ready to eat!

If you make a banana split ...

- What do you do first?

- Where do you put the banana?

- What is poured over the banana and ice cream?

- When do you use the strawberries?

Look at the pictures.

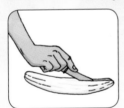   

- Put the instructions in the right order.

Put the strawberries and chocolate chips on the top.

Put the banana on a plate and put the ice cream on top of it.

Pour the chocolate sauce over the banana and ice cream.

Peel the banana and cut it down the middle, from the top to the bottom.

Time for a drink

Copy and complete the sentences.

1 The boy is making a _____.

drink   banana split

2 The boy pours squash into a _____.

mug   glass

3 The boy adds water from the _____.

tap   jug

4 The boy _____ the glass of squash.

drinks   gives away

5 Write a list of what is needed to make a glass of squash.

6 Write instructions for each picture. Here are some words to help.

jug

squash

pour

water

first

drink

glass

then

21

 ## Cooking Sensations

When I see a cookie in the baker's shop
my mouth starts to water and my eyes go pop.

When I hold the cookie in a paper bag
the crackle and the smell start to drive me mad.

But when I bite the cookie and begin to eat
the sound is crunchy and the taste is sweet.

- What is this poem about?
- How do we know the girl wants to eat the cookie?
- Does the cookie smell nice?
- What does the cookie taste like?

Some of the words in the poem rhyme.

- Which word in the poem rhymes with **shop**?
- Which word in the poem rhymes with **eat**?

Read the poem.

Think of actions for the poem.

Read the poem out loud and add your actions.

My mouth starts to water and my eyes go pop.

I Like

I like the taste of toothpaste
tingling on my tongue.

I like the smell of sausages
nuzzling at my nose.

I like the feel of sunshine
flickering on my face.

I like the sound of bells echoing
in my ears.

I like the sight of fairground lights
flashing in the dark.

Copy the right answers.

1 What taste does the boy like?

The taste of toothpaste.   The taste of sausages.

2 What sound does the girl like?

The sound of bells.   The sound of the fairground.

3 What sight does the boy like?

The sunshine flickering.   The fairground lights flashing.

 4 This poem has a line about each of the senses.

> Can you write a poem about the things you <u>don't</u> like?

Write a poem about things you <u>don't</u> like.

Choose some things you don't like to taste, smell feel, hear and see.

Start each line with 'I don't like the ...'

> I don't like the feel of jam slipping through my fingers.

Prince Cinders

Prince Cinders was not much of a prince.

He had three brothers.

They went out a lot.

Prince Cinders had to stay at home.

He wished he was like his brothers.

Then a fairy turned up…

- Is Prince Cinders good-looking?

- How many brothers does Prince Cinders have?

- Where did Prince Cinders' brothers go?

- What fell down the chimney?

What is Prince Cinders like?

- What does he look like?

- Is he happy?

- What would he like to do?

- Which fairy tale is this story like?

- Why do you think this?

Cinderella

Cinderella   I want to go to the ball.

Godmother   I will help you.
You must get home
at 12 o'clock!

Narrator   Cinderella went to the ball.

Prince   I love dancing with you.

Narrator   Cinderella ran from the ball.

Cinderella   I'm late!

Narrator   The shoe fitted.

Prince   I'm so happy.

Narrator   They lived happily ever after.

Copy the right answers.

1 Where did Cinderella want to go?

She wanted to go to the ball.
She wanted to go outside.

2 Who helped Cinderella?

Her sisters helped.
Her godmother helped.

3 Who did Cinderella dance with?

She danced with a friend.
She danced with the prince.

4 Did Cinderella leave the ball on time?

No, she didn't leave on time.
Yes, she left on time.

5 Which story did you like most?

Prince Cinders   Cinderella

Write a sentence saying why.

Remember to use a capital letter and a full stop.

Our visit to the dinosaurs

- Where are the children going?

- Why do you think Jake was crying?

- What made some of the children scream?

- How many horns does a Triceratops have?

Some visits we go on are with our school.

Some are with our family or friends.

- Where have you been on a visit?

    Tell someone else about it. Try to use these words:

    first   then   after   later

My naughty dog!

20th August

My dog Barney is very naughty. He eats shoes! We need to put our shoes away as soon as we take them off so he doesn't eat them.

Yesterday, when Dad came home from work he forgot to put his shoes away. Later, I found Barney chewing Dad's shoes behind the sofa! He looked at me with his big eyes and looked very sorry so I didn't tell him off.

Then I put Dad's shoes away for him. I hope he doesn't see the hole Barney made in them!

Copy and finish the sentences.

1 Barney likes to eat _____ .

books   shoes

2 _____ forgot to put his shoes away.

Dad   Barney

3 Barney chewed the shoes behind the _____ .

cupboard   sofa

4 Barney wasn't told off because he looked _____ .

happy   very sorry

5 Think of something that happened between you and an animal.

Write about what happened.
Remember to write it in the order things happened!

The Sandcastle

Jack liked building sandcastles but he couldn't keep the sea away.

"Stay back, sea!" he said.

"This is my castle; I'm king here."

But it didn't work.

He found a pretty shell and put it on his sandcastle, then made a wish.

He wanted to be king of a real castle.

Jack woke in the night. He looked out of his window and found his wish had come true.

He went to see the castle and was met by a girl.

He went into the castle and the people made him king.

The people danced and danced but didn't hear the water at the door.

Suddenly the water burst in.

The people began to change.

- What does Jack like building?

- What does Jack want to be?

- Who did Jack meet outside the castle?

- What came in through the castle doors?

Some strange things happen in this story.

- Which things wouldn't happen to you in real life?

- What do you think happens next to Jack?

- How do you think the story finishes?

The Tiger Who Came to Tea

Once there was a little girl called Sophie, and she was having tea with her mummy, in the kitchen.
Suddenly there was a ring at the door.
Sophie's mummy said, "I wonder who that can be …We'd better open the door and see."

Sophie opened the door, and there was a big, furry, stripy tiger.
The tiger said, "Excuse me, but I'm very hungry. Do you think I could have tea with you?"
Sophie's mummy said, "Of course, come in."

So the tiger came into the kitchen and sat down at the table.

Sophie's mummy said, "Would you like a sandwich?"
But the tiger didn't take just one sandwich.
He took all the sandwiches on the plate and swallowed them in one big mouthful. Owp!

And he still looked hungry, so Sophie passed him the buns.

The Tiger Who Came to Tea, Judith Kerr

Copy the right answers.

1 Who was Sophie having tea with?

Sophie was having tea on her own.
Sophie was having tea with her mummy.

2 What noise did Sophie hear at the door?

Sophie heard a ring.
Sophie heard a knock.

3 Who opened the door?

Sophie opened the door.
Mummy opened the door.

4 What did the tiger want?

The tiger wanted to meet Sophie.
The tiger wanted to have tea.

 5 These words tell us about Sophie or the tiger.

Copy and sort the words to match the right character.

hungry   small   furry

big         pretty

polite   stripy

Being a friend

Playing on your own
You can play what
you want.

Finding a friend
Sometimes it is more
fun to play with other people.

Playing with friends
You can do many
things, like:
chat,
play chase,
make things,
play football,
race.

- What is this telling us about?

- Is it good to do some things on your own?

- Why do people like playing with friends?

- What things can you do with a friend?

Friends are important.

Look at the sections.

In which section does it tell us:

- what you can do with a friend?

- why it can be good to play by yourself?

- it is fun to play with other people?

The author wants to write more in her book about 'friends'.

- What else could she say?

Sorting out an argument

Here are some steps to help you sort out an argument.

1   Stop arguing.

2   Calm down.
    Take deep breaths.

3   Agree to talk about it.

4   Everyone gets a turn to tell, not yell, their story.

5   Think up lots of ideas to sort out the problem.

6   Choose the best idea, the one everyone agrees with.

7   Do it!

Remember, arguments are allowed, but meanness is not!

Copy and finish the sentences.

1 This _____ tells us what to do if we have an argument.

story   information

2 The first thing you should do is _____ arguing.

stop   keep

3 _____ must have a turn to tell their story.

Everyone   One child

4 Choose the best _____ to solve the argument.

story   idea

5 Have you argued with a friend?

- What was it about?
- Write some sentences saying how you felt and how you sorted it out.

Don't forget to use capital letters and full stops.

41

Cows

Half the time they munched the grass,
  and all the time they lay
Down in the water-meadows, the lazy month of May,
A-chewing,
A-mooing,
To pass the hours away.

- What is the weather like?
- What do the cows have to eat?
- Which cow sees the rain coming?
- Do you think the flies worry the cows?

Listen to the poem again.

- Do you like this poem? Why?
- Do you have a favourite line?

The Cow in the Storm

The sky turned grey,
The horse went 'Neigh',
But the cow just went on chewing.

The sky turned black,
The ducks went 'Quack',
But the cow just went on chewing.

Lightning sparked,
The farm dogs barked,
But the cow just went on chewing.

Raindrops splashed,
The farm cats dashed,
But the cow just went on chewing.

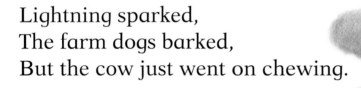

Showers stopped,
Rabbits hopped,
But the cow just went on chewing.

Sunshine streamed,
The whole farm steamed,
But the cow,
The cow,
The cow,
The cow,
But the cow just went on chewing.

Copy the right answers.

1 What is the cow doing?

The cow is sleeping.
The cow is chewing.

2 What sound does the duck make?

Quack
Neigh

3 What do the dogs do?

The dogs dash.
The dogs bark.

4 When does the sun come out?

At the start of the poem.
At the end of the poem.

5 **Rhyming words**

Which word rhymes with:

black?	grey	quack	chewing
barked?	sparked	steamed	dashed
stopped?	neigh	splashed	hopped

6 Which cow poem do you like the best?

How to use this book

This Pupil Book consists of ten units that help to teach comprehension skills for a range of different text types and genres, including fiction, non-fiction and poetry. It can be used as part of the Nelson Comprehension series, which includes Teacher's Resource Books and CD-ROMs. Each Nelson Comprehension unit is split into three sections.

Teach

The 'Teach' section includes an illustrated text or a picture stimulus for a teacher and children to read together and discuss in class. Extended texts and discussion points are supplied in the accompanying *Teacher's Resource Book*, with full multi-modal whiteboard support (complete with voiceovers and a range of audio and visual features) on the CD-ROM.

Talk

The aim of this section is to get the children in small groups to practise the skills they have just learnt. Each child could take on a role within the group, such as scribe, reader or advocate. They are presented with a range of questions to practise the skills they have been learning in the 'Teach' section.

The questions are followed up by a discussion, drama, role play or other group activity to further reinforce their learning. Further guidance is supplied in the *Teacher's Resource Book*, while interactive group activities to support some of the 'Talk' questions and activities are supplied on the CD-ROM.

Write

The third section offers an opportunity to test what the children have learnt by providing a new text extract and a series of questions, which can be answered orally, as a class exercise, or as an individual written exercise. The questions include initial literal questions, followed by vocabulary clarification, inference and evaluation questions and then extended follow-up activities. Full answer guidance and PCMs are supplied in the accompanying *Teacher's Resource Book*, while a whiteboard questioning reviewing feature is supplied on the CD-ROM.

Using the Pupil Book alongside the Nelson Comprehension ICT

The Nelson Comprehension Pupil Book and Teacher's Resource Book for Red level are supported by the Red level CD-ROM which provides fully interactive whole-class whiteboard and group computer activities. The CD-ROM includes each of the units and its extracts and texts, and matches the Teach–Talk–Write structure of the Pupil Book.

Teach

The ICT Teach section supplies the Pupil Book / Teacher's Resource Book extract in a multi-media form – with voiceover, sound effects, images and, in some cases, video or animation. The images and voiceover can be switched on and off in order to increase or remove supports for a child's comprehension. A selection of the questions from the Pupil Book is supplied with the ICT, along with the highlighting of clues in the text, a free-type box for scribing possible answers, and model answers to support the modelling of inferring or deducing an answer. A range of annotation tools is also provided so any new questions or points which the teacher or pupil raise can also be highlighted.

Teach section, Unit 5, CD-Rom, Red

Talk

The ICT Talk section supplements the Pupil Book small group discussion and role-play questions by providing a range of 'Talk activities'. These ICT activities are specially designed to stimulate discussion or support a drama activity in relation to a particular comprehension question. The ICT

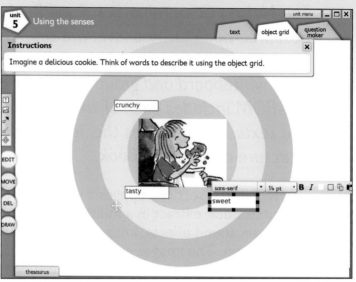

Object grid, Talk section, Unit 5, CD-Rom, Red

activities include: dilemma vote, character grid, story map, information categoriser, sequencer, question maker and a text formatter (which allows children to create their own playscript or other specific text type).

Write

The ICT Write section is designed to provide a whiteboard or desktop reviewing system for children who have completed or are engaged in a class or group discussion of the Write extract and activities in the Pupil Book. As in the Teach section, all the questions are provided, along with selectable clue highlights,

Write section, Unit 8, CD-Rom, Red

a free-type facility and a model answer which gives an idea of a plausible answer to the question. All questions can be hovered over with the mouse to reveal a definition of the type of comprehension question it is.